MEMORIES PRETEND TO SLEEP

THE POETRY OF JULIA GJIKA

Translated from the Albanian by Ani Gjika

Egret

CHAPEL HILL
2020

First Edition

Printed in the United States of America
Cover and book design by Maxine Mills

Laertes

Egret is an imprint of Laertes Press, Incorporated | www.laertesbooks.org

MY MOTHER'S TONGUE: AN INTRODUCTION TO JULIA GJIKA'S POETRY

It's an impossible task to write about translating the poetry of your own mother, and even harder to introduce her poetry to a Western audience. These two challenges have been hovering over my shoulders so that it took me weeks to just sit down and begin. But I have finally found my mother's tongue, and so I begin where she did.

Born in 1949, Julia Gjika grew up during the harshest years of Albania's Communist regime when literature from the West was strictly censored and her own poems often were not allowed in print throughout the 1970s and 1980s. When compared to that of other countries in Europe, women's poetry in Albania is fairly recent. There's a long oral tradition, and Albanian women have been noted through centuries as the primary creators of lullabies and elegies. In fact, the tradition still exists today whereby a woman will be paid to come to a funeral and sing of the life and works of the person who has died. However, women in Albania did not break into print until the 1970s. Julia Gjika belongs to this first generation of female poets, having published her first book, *Ditëlindje* (Birthday) in 1971 followed by *Ku Gjej Poezinë* (Where I Find Poetry) in 1978.

In 1996, Gjika immigrated with her family to the United States. She had stopped writing poetry in 1980, but began writing again in 2000. Her collection, *Muzg: Vëllim Poetik* (Dusk: Collected Poems) where some of these translations come from, was published in 2007. Others are new or taken from her latest collection, *Ëndrra e Kthimit* (The Dream of Returning), which was published in 2010. Gjika's poetry is characterized by an unflinching honesty, precision of thought and language, and the peculiar combination of wisdom with a childlike vulnerability. Her poetry reflects the sacrifices of an immigrant specifically, and the human experience more generally, in a way that is subtle, real, and original.

When I read my mother's poetry, I understand what it means to finally hear my mother's tongue: gentle, unadorned, discerning, the kind of language that transmits a message straight to one's soul. What I also hear very clearly is what she sacrificed when immigrating to the U.S. — poetry and time to sit and be with words. But the thing about being with words is that you can still let them in even while you're doing everything else as long as you don't weaken. So while she spent the last twenty years before retiring cooking at a college cafeteria, cleaning offices and houses, binding magazines and journals into large volumes at a book bindery before and while she was learning English in evening ESL classes, everything Gjika did carried her "toward the dream that never dies." Perhaps that's the dream of returning to Albania, to the people and places she had left. Or more likely, the dream is poetry itself — something that she never abandoned, even though she immigrated at 48 years old, even through the hardships of the physically demanding menial jobs available to her in a rural town in a country whose language she, at first, did not speak.

These two facts give her poetry a unique immigrant's voice. She's the immigrant who worked minimum wage, 39 hours a week, and not 40, so she wouldn't be allowed benefits, but she's also the one who "learned the native tongue/and raised [her] voice" when asking for what was rightfully hers. What is also unique about this voice is that Gjika doesn't shy away from writing about the cost of displacement, depression, isolation — what become an immigrant's first dwelling places. Even without naming any of these states of being, the reader senses them in poems like "Who Are You?," "Nothingness," "Metamorphosis," "Adult Day Care Island," and all the way to the ultimate cost, one's own parent having been left behind in the old country — "an orphan in old age."

A dominant theme in Julia Gjika's poetry is nature as healer. When I think about this, I remember our bookshelves in our home back in Tiranë, Albania in the 1970s and 1980s when I was growing up. I can see my mother's favorite books and can trace this theme back to Rabindranath Tagore and Walt Whitman. Nature and its inhabitants — the butterfly, the hummingbird, geese — become the answers to prayers to someone who's found herself constantly watched by an unidentified, plural "they" that rears its head in poems like "Flowers," "The Red East" where it's the apartments and one's own home that takes its place, "Self-Portrait," and "Voices That Rend" where it's felt the strongest. Gjika's strength is not in directly stating or pointing out what "they" refers to, but in subtly mentioning what can only be perceived as a sure threat — perhaps as certain a presence in the lines as the reality of being surveyed, judged, spied on, and persecuted was in Albania during and after the Communist regime.

When translating Gjika's poems, I was attentive to the rhythms of words within and between the lines. I was particularly attentive to lines where she makes good use of alliteration and wordplay. Perhaps the most challenging example is in the poem "Metamorphosis." In Albanian, the last three lines can be translated literally as: "to the place where I was born/I belong, I don't belong/I burst (or: explode)," however, the words "përkas" and "plas" create an effective rhyme at the end that has an almost onomatopoeic quality that simulates an eruption of sorts. I couldn't simply translate that as "I belong/I don't belong/I burst." I didn't want to introduce a new image, which would change the poem a lot, but as a translator, I had the freedom to slightly modify the line and use other words to connote a slightly different meaning. So while in the original, the poem ends on a negative tone, someone tormented by feeling displaced, "I break into song" is my little *traduttore, tradittore* move, which I find apt for this particular poem and this poet who literally broke into song in the decades following her immigration to the U.S. The life of the Albanian woman up until we left the country in 1996 required Gjika to work hard both to make a living and keep a house. She also refused to betray her artistic expression to advance the party line. For all these reasons, throughout the 1980s and early 1990s Gjika stopped writing poetry. In the U.S., although immigration presented new adversities, she had the freedom to write on any topic, so she wrote — hundreds of poems as a direct result of and response to these new challenges and joys. And while the line "I break into song" is slightly different from the original, it is a testament to how translators, who must rely on deep reading, can sometimes reach beyond what the author could have known initially.

I feel most inspired through translation when I push myself to invent rather than simply imitate the line's structure. In "Third Thoughts on Translating Poetry," Jackson Mathews says that the translator "has to invent formal effects in his own language that give a sense of those produced by the original in its own . . . The usual mistake is to believe that the form of the model must somehow be copied." I think I was successful at reinventing the form of Gjika's "Memories" where I had to play around with which words could go in one line and how the poem had to end. Most of the lines in the original are one-word lines, but because Albanian is an inflected language, and those single words are verbs, their suffixes imply an action upon the subject that they modify. So instead of translating, in the second stanza, "bug one another/hurt one another," I rearranged those lines to read: "taunt and hurt/one another." Using two verbs in one line intensifies the action that is being described without losing the effect. A little earlier in the same stanza, the words "fërfëllojnë" and "bisedojnë" rhyme and simply mean "quiver" and "talk/chat," so to create the illusion of rhythm instead of rhyme, I used a similar line structure for both lines, "how they quiver/how they flirt." I tried, as Dryden recommended in his "Preface to *Ovid's Epistles,*" "to vary but the dress" sometimes without changing or completely losing the substance of the original text. In "A Prayer," the literal translation of line five is: "neither like a heavy lady," "heavy" meaning someone pretentious, snobby. The last word in that line, "zonjë," is really the equivalent of the French word "madame," so I took some liberties in translating that line as "neither may I become a pompous/old dame."

My mother has often told me about how, when she was pregnant with me, she had to crawl under parked freight trains, just before dawn, to get to work on time on the other side of the railroad tracks. This is the subject of the poem that opens this collection, "My Train." How poignant for me to read now what she thought of back then: "When will my baby rest?" To think of her those early mornings, alone, crawl-crossing railroad tracks with me inside her, to then together move to the United States and struggle with what an immigrant struggles with the most — "I don't know who I am" — at least initially, to now being able to bring her work to a larger audience in a larger language than Albanian, makes it seem all worth it. The truth is, no sacrifice is worth it unless you transform yourself in the process, and in that I do find rest.

It is my mother who writes about people who are rendered invisible in the process of transitioning to a new life in another country: "the aging adults who migrated after middle age." It is my mother who transformed her life, the one who worked silently so her children got their higher educations and her husband wrote and published his books. She reminds me of Wisława Szymborska who asks, "But what is poetry anyway?" only to answer, "I just keep on not knowing, and I cling to that/like a redemptive handrail." Julia Gjika is a poet who, like the child who puts her ear to the railroad track to hear her train coming, has felt everything deeply, and given herself permission in the face of it all to "break into song." May we all have such strength and courage.

---

1. Matthew Jackson, "Third Thoughts on Translating Poetry," *On Translation*, (Boston: Harvard University Press, 1959), 67–77.

2. Rainer Schulte and John Biguenet, Ed., *Theories of Translation*, (Chicago: University of Chicago Press, 2012), 154.

3. Wisława Szymborska, "Some Like Poetry," *The New Republic*, October 28, 1996, https://newrepublic.com/article/100289/some-people-poetry.

MY TRAIN

I have waited at train stations, alone,

at times jostling through, among strangers, to find a seat.

Then the alarm whistle pierced the heavens

shuffling countless scenes before my eyes.

The rhythm of train wheels would follow me till I'd get off.

I've waited for my train with my belly round — up to my mouth.

My face beaten by the cold rain of impatience: When would my baby rest?

When the platform was blocked by freight trains,

my train was late. Heavy on my feet, I'd sigh

wanting to go back to the street, my home already vanished.

On hands and feet, I'd crawl, my belly to my mouth, under freight trains,

anxious of the smallest move until my foot touched the asphalt.

My train was full of smiling children riding to school.

A slice of corn bread sprinkled with sugar and water in their gelid hands.

Under their armpits, textbooks wrapped in bags of cloth,
and, as if chewed up by mice, torn corners
spit out pencils and erasers — breadcrumbs to guide them back.
My train heavy with long years of labor
and the long daily ledger of accounts. Millions spent
on building bunkers ordered by the head of construction.
Orders on top of other orders, the last one from the stern commander
who'd come to work drunk every morning.
At train stations, alone, I've waited,
with my belly to my mouth, for my train.
The pristine landscape would fly past me
holding me spellbound, hypnotized.
My train — through the locomotive's whistle that signaled an arrival,
the noise, and the rhythm of wheels on rails —
went on snatching my youth completely, seamlessly.

THE BOYS OF MY STREET

Their bodies intoxicated with fresh air.
They grow twice as fast through triumphs,
marveling at nature
and water gurgling down the mountain.
The boys of my street
used to return home
like warriors after battle
when dusk fell,
tired from their games,
setting traps in the fields,
hunting birds with slingshots.
They delighted
in the life of the bird quivering in their hands
until it spent.
Satisfied
when over a bonfire
of sticks and whatever else they'd gathered
the soft flesh roasted as cinders scorched.
Delighted, the boys of my street
savored the moist meat,
chucking left and right on the green grass

delicate bones soft as the feathers.
Nobody ever queried
the sky above, enfolding, growing dark.
The sky waited for its residents,
for the music of wings
to sound on high.
The boys of my street
by accident, while playing,
became bandits.

FLOWERS

I seal shut,
shrink,
I become a fist,
a bud
in your hand.
Your touch
opens me again.
I swell,
I bloom into a rose.
They pluck me.
To pluck a rose —
why is it such a thrill?!

FOOTPRINTS THAT TALK

A head for a head!
So would a thief absolve his soul
since the days of Ali Pashë Tepelena.[1]
At times he had a nickname,
at times his fame preceded him
like strange red greenbacks three hours away.
He never slept without a loaded gun under his pillow.
Without it, he'd never go on the road "to hunt."

In the five-star Hotel Arts in Barcelona,
where worldwide famous celebrities vacation
the likes of Mick Jagger, Eric Clapton, Cindy Crawford,
a few years ago the grand theft of the century took place.
Some general had precious objects stolen.
Halal! some said. *They've taken the rich man's excess.*
Haram! said others when the police caught the thief.

1. Ali Pashë Tepelena was the Ottoman Albanian ruler from the 1700s until 1820 when he died.

According to legend, the god Pan died in Butrint.[2]
The nature spirits wailed
so shepherds everywhere would hear
of the tragic loss. Who would protect the forests,
the flowers in years to come?
To this day
the axe of a thief flattens them and won't stop.

Insidious night, taciturn.
The moon hidden in the dark sky.
Not even the leaves in the chestnut forest stirred.
Man slept deeply in his first sleep.
Thieves, as if carrying their footfalls in their arms,
stole six sheep from my grandfather's barn.

My grandfather's howl pierced the dawn
waking up the entire village.
Under a different sky his heart was trembling.
How would he feed his children now?
Those six sheep, the only wealth, were his God.
May the thief's hand be blessed![3] some said to console him.

---

2. Considered a microcosm of Mediterranean history with ruins from ancient Greece, Rome, and Byzantium, Butrint is also a wildlife sanctuary.

3. *Pastë dorën e mbarë!* an Albanian wish after someone's goods are stolen so that whoever took them may have been the last and the suffering may end there.

A thief covers his tracks, but they still talk.
And only God knows if one profits from stolen goods.
After a short time, my grandmother died.
Twice the family was impoverished.
A jinxing hand, like a strong wind that takes the roof off,
stole joy from that house
leaving poverty behind as an inheritance.

THE RED EAST

Apartments. Apartments
of red brick
or concrete.
Same old style
all through the East:
one bedroom,
one living room,
one bathroom,
one balcony;
two bedrooms,
one living room,
one bathroom,
one balcony;
three bedrooms,
one living room,
one bathroom,
one balcony.
A family of eight
or nine children,
one or two elderly in-laws,
the mother, the father.
Good God,
life in communism —

astir in a chicken coop.
Heartbroken,
the woman of the house
washed and swept,
herself unwashed,
cooking in the bathroom
sleeping in the kitchen
the bedroom a storage room
she couldn't breathe in.
Was this the promise
of eating
with a golden spoon?
The apartments
had ears,
wide mouths; the apartments had eyes.
When you opened your mouth,
they could see deep
into your intestines,
your liver.
Your neighbors
had taken inventory
of all the junk in your stomach.
Those apartments
would sell you
for two bucks.

A PRAYER

I search for something in the elderly.
Perhaps myself, after many years.
May I not turn out to be frail
or have to walk around with a cane.
Neither may I become a pompous old dame
tangled up in jewels and gold
all over my hands and neck.
I want to resemble a butterfly —
so light in youth and in old age.
Grant me the aging of butterflies, God,
who remain themselves through their days.

ALONE INSIDE FOUR WALLS

for my father

Inside four walls, my father
lies down on the sofa
for hours.
He gets up, just to stretch his limbs,
looks out the window —
red bricks of another building.
He enters each cold bedroom,
speaks to dumb objects.
Out on the balcony,
he touches the green leaves of geraniums,
happy to find flowers again,
plucks the red chilies he'll love
in the winter with his beans,
each minute
looks at the clock that has stopped working.
When someone calls him,
he talks like a child who's gotten lost.
Who is there with you? I ask him.
No one, who else?
Did anyone drop by today?

A week ago, my sister

with her old age.

What do you do all day?

I look at albums, he says and smiles.

I have all of you in the albums, my wife, my children,
my children's children,

I need a few more of them . . .

When someone knocks on the door,

he doesn't hear it,

even if he did

he wouldn't believe

that someone knocks for him.

My father, now an orphan in old age.

WHAT CANNOT CHANGE

I try to write
but all the more I erase
and further ache.
We lost one another.
Relatives became strangers,
with strangers we've gotten close.
I search for someone
whose face might resemble my mother's.
Sometimes I find the color of her hair
but not how she'd comb it.
A young woman on the street
tall and slender like my sister
without my sister's voice.
An elderly man
pensive like my father,
but his footsteps don't make the sounds
my father's did.
I search for what's mine.
It remains out of reach.
That's why I write
even though I erase
even though I ache.

METAMORPHOSIS

I don't know who I am.
Tell me, please,
who am I?
I no longer recognize myself,
I don't look like me.
Is this me?
I wear someone else's clothes,
I've learned to speak in another's tongue.
Every morning
when I face myself
in the mirror, we ask one another:
Tell me,
do you recognize this face?
This is my face.
Mirror, mirror,
I don't recognize this plastic.
I know I'm me.
I look like me, I don't look like me;
to the country where I was born,
I belong, I don't belong —
I break into song.

SELF-PORTRAIT

Some talk dirt about me
whirling their wet tongues.
Scant blades of grass in love
with their own shadow.
I laugh,
glisten with the stars.
We remember you,
some others say.
When you were young, beautiful,
you wrote sweet poetry.
I look at my hands.
How sensitive they are still.

WHAT AM I DOING HERE?

What am I doing here?
This isn't a dream;
this world had no use for me.
What am I doing here?
Without my homeland —
good as a stump.
Why are we here?
We came to fill our pockets,
without intending to, emptied our hearts.

RAISE YOUR VOICE!

Today, I lost my job
because I opened my mouth.
If I didn't speak the language,
I wouldn't have told my boss
that she was mistaken
and had forgotten to pay me.
She preferred me when I was mute,
but I learned the native tongue
and raised my voice.

APPROACHING SIXTY

You still tell me I'm beautiful.
Don't you see my wrinkles?
Don't you see I'm growing old?
I smooth out your gray hairs,
how they've multiplied,
even worse, my head — a white
lamb — continues to dream.
Our bed is still in the woods,
covered by shrubs, violets,
the scent of cedar.
Birds come to wake us each morning,
dew opens our eyes.
Along each street we walk, your arm
holds me tight.
In crowds, my eyes find you;
among a thousand, I recognize your pace.
We've just crossed middle age,
and I still search
for the lit candle in your mind.

NOTHINGNESS

Nothingness springs up anywhere
waiting for no green light.
Pokes its nose, eavesdrops on a being.
Upon a shadow that stretches in the dark
Nothingness builds disbelief.
Nothingness ravages on.
A frog jumps out, scares Nothingness away.
Nothingness listens in,
turns the seconds heavy,
on the hours of being,
tramples mercilessly.

MEMORIES

Memories
pretend to sleep.
I don't touch them,
I don't stir them.
If they open their eyes,
they'll remind me
I'm a slave.

Let them lie
in a daze.
How they quiver,
how they flirt
with consciousness,
taunt and hurt
one another,
till thrashing,
with gloves off,
they turn on themselves.

IN CONVERSATION WITH MYSELF

I don't have enough faith
to die for what I believe in.
I go to the hospital regularly, once a month.
There are people there who've lost their limbs.
Their piercing eyes
say: *Everyone survives, so do we!*
Once a month, I go to the town cemetery
to remember those that have gone;
I light a candle, plant something new.
You can't wake anyone there.
I don't have enough faith
to die for what I believe in.
A voice tells me: *Wait!*

WHO ARE YOU?

I didn't get to be famous.
I didn't even add a river's blue line
to the world map.
I didn't become anything,
didn't rock the world
even when I bore children.
I wasn't a role model
to anyone.
Stuck in my skin,
counting my losses
so eagerly —
who are you?

DON'T COME ANY CLOSER!

Don't come any closer — said Pride,
First thing that'll happen,
you'll smash your jaws
then lose your name.
Others will mock you.
But I was blind
and crawled on hands and knees
so I could touch her
even if just her toenails.
Life craved Pride
even as I kept losing myself.

LICE SEASON

It's the season when lice race up the oak bark
at dizzying speeds
all the way to the top where birds worship the skies.
It's the season where everywhere their presence stuns.
The ambition to be first,
no, to be supreme.
It's the season that doesn't resemble
the promised season of change
but a whole different one, of deception.
When freedom is overrun.
Like an iron curtain an impossibility hangs,
the impossibility to wipe out nits before they hatch.
A river in Canada
recently turned green.
It wasn't the reflection of the trees,
but a transformation.
Lice, too, are transforming,
self-proclaiming they resemble birds,
seeking wings, threatening to cover the sun.
What a season!

And now they've heard of a St. Valentine
roaming the world
who keeps love constant.
They learn to croon a love song
as they swarm all over freedom.

VOICES THAT REND

I don't want to know about those people anymore
who inside the same country all play judge.
I don't want to know about those
who, under the same roof, open a court case,
having come from the same belly.
I purposely want to slam the door
and shut them out. I know they'll be enraged
like livid wolves in the blizzard,
their howls piercing the frosted chill.
I want to know about the smell of the ocean
that could heal my terror. I want to know
about the stars shining above. I want to hear
the wind's voice, not the voices that rend.
I want to know if my own blood supports me.
I know for centuries foreigners kept the boot on
  our neck.
My heart chokes on questions I have no answers for.
Why are we so spiteful, we people of the Balkans,
from deep within our blood?

DREAMING WITH EYES WIDE OPEN

When I was small,
I used to paint the same house —
two or three gables,
large windows with red shutters,
and a small path
winding to the garden.
Grass and flowers all around,
trees, and a sun in the blue sky.
Growing up,
with eyes wide open,
I dreamed of having my own roof.
I got all of it
when there was no time to plant any flowers.

HOMETOWN TIES

Every night, I'm somewhere else,
and I forget the roof I'm under.
Locked in some kind of cell
without handcuffs, without prison guards.
Every night, I'm somewhere else,
and I forget the roof I'm under.
The big house, the loud noises;
its voices hold me hostage.

AUTUMN AFTERNOON

The sun was setting just as I'd finished cleaning
the offices of a two-story building,
ending another day of work
near the dumpster
with the last bag of trash I tossed away.
I was alone with my exhaustion.
You could hear nobody's footsteps.
Somewhere between my exhaustion and a faded dream,
I thought I was lost,
when suddenly in the gloaming
the flight of the wild geese —
I raised my head.
Their white bellies
glided through the numerous hues
the firmament had stolen from the season.
In an instant, exhaustion and rest became one.
The green, blue, pink, amber-gold hues
and the sounds calling from the birds' beaks
carried me toward the dream
that never dies.
How hard it is to believe

that after a tiring, monotonous day
which you forget in a night's sleep,
dusk opened a window,
so I could see
what my memory
safekeeps.

ADULT DAY CARE ISLAND

Aged adults gather each morning
on their own island,
playing carefree,
convinced that one day they'll leave it all behind.
They like to walk on their own two feet,
one holding on to a cane,
another his nephew by the hand.
Lorenci's coffee waits for them.
He offers them a variety: Turkish, espresso,
Americano, then sweets, ice cream.

Lorenci's father left, says Vangjel,
he went back to the old country.
Same thing happened to Nasi's father,
decades ago, he left America.
His mother sent for him to get him married.
He was 16 when he arrived here, 27 when he left.
Before my spit dries on the sidewalk, his mother told him,
come back, I'm waiting for you here at the doorstep!
He went back to Albania, but the borders closed.
Today, those of us who've come here, rarely go back.

This is migration for us,
not like their exile, a century ago.

I can't sleep, they complain to one another.
At night, in the moon's mirror,
they see their own faces,
laughing on the spot at their old age.
Each one with their own loneliness
pulls together for the final stretch.
With their heads turned back, souls never at peace,
they speak at the same time, can't wait for their turn.
The aging adults who migrated after middle age.

Before I let go, says Vangjel,
I'll tell my sons
to take me back to my hometown, Korca,
where my body can rest near my own people.
And then proudly, in one voice, they talk about
nieces and nephews, achievements America gave them.
They love it at Lorenci's. They're his father's friends.
Ah, if only there was death without aging,
the ancient wish rises to the clouds.
Relieved, they return to their sons' or daughters' houses,
fully convinced that in the end only the best awaits them.

THE FACE OF AN ELDERLY MAN SMILES AT ME

November 1.
All night the livid wind blew.
The streets awoke clothed in golden leaves.
All night the rain washed and rinsed them clean.
Under this autumn sky, an aging man walks slowly.
He smiles at me this morning,
gold shadows reflecting in his eyes,
eyebrows thin like wires.
He walks slowly holding a rose in his hands.
I stop in front of him, not wanting to let him out of my sight.
We stand face to face in the middle of the road.
He doesn't say a word, yet I know what he's telling me.
I give him my hand to get him on the sidewalk,
the only service I can offer him and just for a few moments.
I hold his ice-cold palm
where the rose is nestled warm.

THE HOUSE AMONG THE PINES

This is a quiet house, a hundred years old;
behind closed blinds, the rooms stilled as if by endless sleep,
perhaps recalling the past by the fireplace,
where ash from winters long gone has grown cold.
Locked doors, moths everywhere, dry wings in every corner,
on couches, in cold rooms seeking warmth from the morning light.
Spiders, unreeling filament,
weave in sheer freedom elaborate, transparent traps.
Still life on the walls and portraits of writers in black and white
from centuries ago.
The portrait of Walt Whitman facing north
where, in sunlight, his beard and hair glisten down to the roots.
I hear a phone ring, as if they're calling me from another time.
They announce
that I have won a cruise ticket to the Caribbean islands.
Spam of the moment, business from the 21st century. I don't answer it.
I quiet myself to be attuned to the house.
Few friends visit here, and then rarely.

The way it keeps hundred-year-old stories hidden,

it will also keep the story of the bird that visited me once,

strangely so close to my face

as I stood on the fire escape watching the half-lights of the evening.

The next day, the house broke its silence;

the messenger had brought along a ray of light that defied the blinds.

I made an effort not to drag my foot though in pain from chronic arthritis.

All around the buzz of bees, butterflies, dragonflies, wasps

who'd made their nests on the roof.

Bats came early, before dawn,

like thieves who cover their tracks.

The house broke the silence spun of meaninglessness

the day the hummingbird king called on me.

ACKNOWLEDGMENTS

Thanks to the editors of the following publications in which some of these translations first appeared (sometimes in different forms):

Asymptote: "Hometown Ties," "Autumn Afternoon," "Footprints that Talk," "The Boys of My Street," "The House Among the Pines"; *Two Lines Online:* "In Conversation with Myself," "Don't Come Any Closer!" "Who Am I?"; *236 Magazine:* "The Red East," "Memories"; *Taos Journal of International Poetry and Art:* "Lice Season," "My Train"; *Burgeon Online:* "What Cannot Change"; *Gobshite Quarterly:* "Prayer," "Raise Your Voice!"

Much gratitude to Rosanna Warren in whose class I first began to translate my mother's poetry ten years ago. My deepest thanks to my editor, Nina Kamberos, who truly pushed me and whose attentive readings helped make this collection sing.

My deepest appreciation and gratitude is for my parents for everything they've taught me about the value of work worth doing.

The following poems were taken from the collection *Dusk*, published in 2007.

Memories

Metamorphosis

Adult Day Care Island

The Face of an Elderly Man Smiles at Me

What Cannot Change

Alone Inside Four Walls

Hometown Ties

Raise Your Voice!

What am I Doing Here?

Prayer

Flowers

The following poems were taken from the collection *The Dream of Returning*, published in 2010.

- Approaching Sixty
- Self-portrait
- The Red East
- In Conversation with Myself
- Who Are You?
- Don't Come Any Closer!
- Dreaming with Eyes Wide Open

Other poems like "My Train," "The Boys of My Street," "Lice Season," "Autumn Afternoon," "The House Among the Pines," "Voices That Rend," "Emptiness," "Footprints that Talk" are recent and haven't yet been published in book form.